10-3-15

*Many thanks to my wife, Patience, for her encouragement in the process of writing this book.*

*I appreciate my children ( Courage, Linda, and Anthony ) for the critical roles they played in the publication of this book. Courage spent countless hours transcribing my voice into written words. Then, she spent more time in carefully reviewing the manuscript. Linda and Anthony read several versions of the book and offered constructive comments.*

*I am grateful to the following individuals for reading my manuscript and making helpful suggestions: Julie Calvalho, Katherine Mercurio Gotthardt, Laura Carrol, Betty Covington, Milt Johns, Allison Nourse-Miller.*

*Finally, I would like to thank my parents for instilling in me the values of hard work and perseverance.*

*Many thanks to my second grade teacher, Dr. Isaac Elimimian, for showing me how to use the power of praise to bring out the best in children.*

*You can contact me at motaigbe@gmail.com.*

Mascot Books
560 Herndon Parkway #120
Herndon, VA 20170
info@mascotbooks.com

Library of Congress Control Number: 2014918599

PRBVG0715A

ISBN-13: 9781620867068

Printed in the United States

# www.mascotbooks.com

# ABCs

## of Creating an Academic Star

How to Bring Out the Genius in Your Child

## Dr. Michael I. Otaigbe

### illustrations by
## Alberto Massetti

# ABCs

## of Creating an Academic Star

How to Bring Out the Genius in Your Child

# Attend your child's school functions

Back-to-school nights, parent-teacher conferences, student performances, and other scheduled meetings with teachers are all opportunities to solidify your involvement. Attending these shows your child that you are serious about education. It shows your child that you are serious about her doing well in school. It gives you the opportunity to get to know teachers and principals who are more likely to give special attention to your child after seeing your commitment.

Exchange phone numbers and e-mail addresses with your child's teachers. Tell the teachers to contact you when your child begins to exhibit bad behavior. Assure the teachers that you prefer to nip bad behavior in the bud before it gets out of hand. When you get home, go over the rules and expectations with your child. This review will reinforce what the teachers covered in class and demonstrate that you and the teachers are on the same page. Moreover, your child is less likely to misbehave when she knows you have a relationship with members of the faculty and administration.

# Become a cheerleader for your child's academic success

Celebrate academic achievement and good behavior in school. Promote a culture within your home in which good performance in school is rewarded. In my house, I made a big deal out of good grades. You don't have to wait for midterm grades or interim reports. If you see a good grade brought home, make a big deal out of it. Call all in the house together and show it to them. Your child will feel so good about himself and will want to continue to make you proud.

As you celebrate academic achievement, don't forget to also celebrate good behavior in school. Academic success and good behavior go hand in hand. In my opinion, you can't have one without the other. In fact, I placed more emphasis, to the dismay of my kids, on the far right-hand corner of the grade report that contained student conduct. I believe that when behavior is good, the grades will follow. Children cannot get good grades if homework is not handed in, they talk too much, or do not follow the teacher's instructions. We know how to celebrate success in other ways, such as cheering during a soccer match. Why not do that for academics?

# Cooperate with your child's teachers and school staff

First, make sure that your child knows you will not tolerate insubordination towards the teachers and school staff. Make sure your child knows that when she goes to school, her focus should be on her books and not on disrespecting the teacher. I used to tell my children that the teacher is always right. Sometimes, this might not be quite true. However, my children wouldn't say they were not doing well because their teacher didn't like them. That was my way of removing that excuse.

Second, if a teacher asks you for a meeting, do what you need to do to accommodate the teacher's request. This includes canceling appointments or taking time off from work to meet with the teacher so that your child will excel in school.

Third, volunteer to help in the classroom. Volunteer to chaperone your child's field trips. This will communicate to your child how important education is.

# Don't compare one child's performance with another's

Compare your child's performance to his prior performance, not to a sibling's or other person's performance. Say something like, "When you were in the fourth grade, you were making all A's. You were very good at math. What did you do then when you were making those A's?" That's a more productive discussion than making lazy comparisons like, "Why don't you be like so and so?" Saying, "Hey, at one point in your life, you were very good in this subject - what happened? What did you do at that time that made you so good in that particular subject?" is more empowering than just comparing your child to his sibling(s).

Children learn differently. One child may learn best through auditory learning, while another child may learn best through visual learning. Yet another child may learn best through doing things (tactile learning). Therefore, it is not fair to your child to compare him to a sibling.

# Encourage your child to do well in challenging courses

It's human nature to give up when the going gets rough. We adults give up when something gets too difficult, and so do children. It is important to encourage your child to take challenging classes and do well in them. I tell everybody I know that it's better to get a lower grade in a challenging subject such as physics or math than to get an A in an easy subject. By going through the challenging class, your child is preparing for college work.

The student who goes through a calculus class in high school is more likely to feel comfortable in a higher-level math class in college than the student who got an easy A in an easier math class. Going through challenging classes will prepare your child for admission into challenging majors that will lead to a better job and better future.

# Form a study group
# of eager learners

Why not form a neighborhood study group of young people who are motivated to do well in school? Make sure you make it fun for them. Provide popcorn or ice cream so that they will enjoy coming back and participating in the study group. One day, it could be math. Another day, it could be writing. A third day, it could be science.

A group like this will really help the young people become grounded in their classes and look forward to going back to school the following week. Forming a study group also lets students know they are not the only ones struggling in a particular area and that no one knows the subject without putting in the work to learn. It brings home the idea that they, in turn, have to work hard to be good at anything.

# Get your child a library card and help him use it

One of the great advantages of living in the United States is the free access to libraries. A library card provides access to all kinds of books, audio programs, DVDs, and CDs. If you want to learn a language, your neighborhood library might have an audio program that you can borrow. There's no excuse not to get an education because everybody has access to the library. The library also has computers that can be used to access the Internet, which opens more doors to learning. Encourage your child to use a library card.

# Hire a tutor to bring your child up to speed or to get ahead

Even teachers have a misconception that children have to be failing to hire a tutor. This is far from true. You should hire a tutor even when your child is not struggling. A tutor can help your child get grounded in the class and then get ahead. When students are failing, they are probably already discouraged and more likely to see the hiring of a tutor as punishment. It's better to arrange a tutor before your child is having problems in school.

You don't have to spend a lot of money when hiring a tutor. You could start with your neighborhood school to find out which teacher wants to do some tutoring on the side. You may also find a high-achieving high school student who can bring your child up to speed. Think of it as an investment in success.

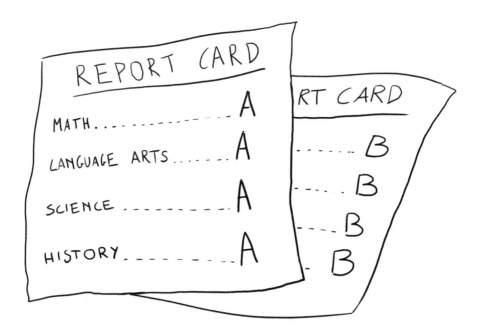

# Insist on academic excellence

A popular quote says, "Shoot for the moon. Even if you miss, you'll land among the stars." Encourage your child to shoot for a 100% score. 95% or 90% is okay. But if she shoots for 90% at the beginning, she may not even get a 90%. That's why it's important for your child to shoot high and continue to work towards it. If she aims for a C, she may end up getting a failing grade.

You can search for good role models for your child to meet. Maybe there's someone you know taking advanced placement classes or there's a student who's participating in a dual enrollment program (in high school and also taking college classes). That student can tell your child how to prioritize schoolwork and achieve academic excellence.

# Join the PTA at
# your child's school

By joining the Parent Teacher Association, you're interacting with the school staff, including the teachers and the principal, so that they know you and your child. They are more likely to tell you when your child is misbehaving before it becomes serious. Your participation in PTA activities will make your presence known in the school, which is good for you and your child.

# Know your child's favorite activities

Knowing your child's favorite activities will help you have conversations outside of academics. It will also help you know when your child may want to watch television so you don't schedule studying at that time. When you show an interest in something dear to your child, he is more likely to bond with you and listen to you when you introduce other topics, like the need to study hard in school.

When you know the characters of your child's favorite show, you can zero in on some of them and tie in examples from the show to illustrate points like never giving up and doing your best in school. These points will really hit home with your child.

Moreover, if you know what your child is watching, you can monitor it to make sure it isn't sending the wrong message. When you know your child's favorite television shows, you can also introduce him to shows and movies with positive messages based on your knowledge of what he likes.

My son, who in high school was interested in public speaking, won the Virginia Championship in Forensics. I use it to motivate him for academic success. I remind him that he didn't get there in one day. He participated in several forensic tournaments. Sometimes he placed, and other times he did not, but he never gave up. He kept learning and presenting himself to different judges, reading their criticisms and comments, and adjusting his speaking accordingly. Learning about my son's interests helped me to zero in on what he likes and use it to motivate him for academic success.

# Listen to your child

You have to hear your child's viewpoint on certain things. It shouldn't be a one-sided communication approach. I must confess that I wasn't good in this department. My children will tell you that I did not always listen to their points of view. But over the years, I found that if you take the time to listen to them, they are more likely to listen to you. They are more likely to hear you if you are willing to hear their viewpoints.

When your child comes home and says a particular subject is difficult, hear him out. Why is it difficult? Listening to your child's struggles will make it easier to help him find solutions. Don't minimize what your child says. Don't brush it off as, "Oh, you just have to do this and this, and that's it."

Listen to your child so that you can figure out the source of the issue. Is it lack of sleep? Is it where he is sitting in the classroom? Maybe there are a lot of distractions in a particular area. Your child may tell you he doesn't like his teachers. Find out why. Ask him what the teachers do that he doesn't like. If you don't ask questions and listen, you won't get all this information - information that will help you help your child overcome obstacles to achieving academic success.

# Motivate your child to get through frustration and discouragement

A part of learning is being frustrated and discouraged. It is very easy to get frustrated with learning, especially with new material. If you expose your child to the theories behind learning new material, he will excel in school.

Jerry Useem told *Fortune Magazine* in 2006 about levels of excellence. When we're learning new things, we go through several levels.

The first level is unconscious incompetence - we don't know what we don't know. Your child does not know that he does not know fractions.

The second level is conscious incompetence - we know what we don't know. Your child is then introduced to fractions and is now aware that he doesn't know fractions.

The third level is conscious competence - we accumulate knowledge through practice. Your child plugs away at learning how to do fractions by solving fraction after fraction.

The fourth level is unconscious excellence - we have mastered the subject, and it comes easily to us. As your child keeps practicing, he comes to master solving fractions.

The last level is conscious excellence - we can successfully explain the subject to others. Your child now knows fractions well enough to successfully explain to others how to do them.

Share this theory with your child. You need to teach your child that learning new material or a new subject can be frustrating, but there are ways to get over the frustration, namely, being patient with himself as he goes through the levels. Once your child knows this, he will know how to get over discouragement and frustration that comes with the learning process.

One thing you should remind your child to keep in mind is not to become overconfident after reaching conscious excellence - that's how silly mistakes are made.

# No television, computers or video games in the bedroom

You may think your child has gone to bed, but she may actually be playing video games, be on the computer, or be watching television until two or three in the morning. If school starts at 7 a.m., she will be tired. This tiredness may affect her attitude and conduct in school.

Some children have smartphones, but parents should be mindful that electronics should not get in the way of their children going to school refreshed and ready to learn.

# Over-learning the material should be stressed

Encourage your child to study the material to the point that it becomes a part of him. In math, no way exists to learn to this extent other than attempting more problems. Have your child work as many problems as possible. If he runs out of problems in the textbook, purchase another book related to the material to allow him to solve some more. Look for websites online that have practice problems. After he has solved 500 or 1,000 math problems, the material becomes a part of him to the point where he can just lie down and solve equations in his head.

# Praise your child for good conduct in school

As parents, we are more likely to scold a child when we hear from the school about bad behavior than to praise him for not getting into trouble. Once in a while, tell your child, "You know, I haven't heard any bad reports about your behavior from school for a long time. I haven't received any phone call that says you have not listened to your teacher. I'm proud of you."

Do that so your child will remember that when the temptation comes in school to behave badly, you are proud of his good conduct. Also, once in a while, praise your child if teachers are saying good things about him. Let your child know, "Mr. Smith was praising you today when I visited your school. He told me how wonderful you are and how well you conduct yourself." Make sure you tell your child because knowing will positively affect his behavior in school. A behavior rewarded is more likely to be repeated.

When I was little, my mom once said to me, "I was at the store today, and I came across some elders. They were talking about you. They were telling me how well behaved you are. They told me how you were the first to greet them and how you gave up your seat for an elderly man." This praise was music to my ears. Since I was not sure which elders were talking wonderfully about me, I made sure I treated every elder I came across with dignity and respect.

THERE IS NO SUCH THING AS A STUPID QUESTION!

# Questions should be encouraged

When a child is growing up, he is full of questions. "What is this?" "What is that?" "Why is the sky blue?" "Why is the sun shining?" "How do you know there is God?" Here is a question my eldest daughter, Courage, asked me over twenty years ago, which still keeps me awake at night: "Do you think in English or Esan, your native language?" I am still thinking of the correct answer to that question.

Children are naturally curious. Make sure you don't give the impression that your child is bothering you with questions. Otherwise, he will stop asking questions. Isn't that what we do as adults? The child asks questions, and through body language or tone, we tell him that we don't condone asking questions or being curious. Before you know it, the child gets the message and stops asking questions. Then we wonder why he is not curious. We were the ones who scared it out of him!

Even when you feel you have answered a question a hundred times, answer it again with a tone of voice that says you appreciate an inquisitive mind. Say with enthusiasm, "That's a good question! Keep them coming because I am learning from them as well." Or you can say, "Let's research that question together."

Practice academic honesty at all times. Never try to save face by giving false answers. Simply say, "I do not have the answer to that question. Perhaps we could look it up online."

Let's encourage questions from our children and give them the freedom to question our answers. As the Chinese proverb clearly states, "He who asks a question is a fool for five minutes; he who does not ask a question remains a fool forever."

# Read to your child

Research studies have shown that children who are read to at an early age develop a higher aptitude for learning in general. They are more likely to have higher-level critical thinking skills. They concentrate and behave better in class. Therefore, it is important you develop the habit of reading to your child at an early age. If the habit is not planted early, your child is likely to develop other habits, such as watching television or playing mindless video games.

When you read to your child, she feels a connection and it becomes a habit. Before you know it, your child will love reading. It doesn't have to take too much of your time. Fifteen minutes a day is enough. The important thing is that you have to do it often, and you have to do it with joy.

Be a role model by reading yourself. In my household, I try to set the example. My children can feel the joy that I feel when a new issue of *Time*, *The Economist*, or *Foreign Affairs* magazine arrives in the mail. They can see it when I pick up the *Financial Times* or *The Wall Street Journal* from the driveway. They can see it when I curl up near the fireplace re-reading African novels such as *Things Fall Apart* by Chinua Achebe or *The African Child* by Camara Laye. Sometimes as I read, I verbalize the joy I derive from reading. I say aloud, "I just love reading. Reading takes me to far away places to learn about the economy, politics, and culture of other people."

As your child grows older, you can have her read to you. I used to play a wonderful game with my son. When I was taking him to school, I brought along a book, magazine, or newspaper and said something like, "Since I can't read and drive at the same time, would you be kind enough to read me the headlines in today's *Financial Times*?" After an initial pushback, he relented, and we usually ended up having a spirited discussion about financial news.

# S is for snow days and learning in a fun way

If your child's school is closed due to snow, don't worry too much about learning loss. A recent Harvard University study has confirmed that no significant learning loss takes place as a result of school closure due to inclement weather. Many school districts have built additional school days into their calendars in anticipation of treacherous weather conditions.

When it snows, try your best to relax. Join the kids in the excitement. Run outside with them; dance, jump, and play! As you begin to have fun outside, sneak in some math and chemistry lessons (but don't call them that) by making snow pyramids and collecting, measuring, and comparing snowflakes. Then go inside to create and tell stories about snow days. Serve popcorn and ice cream to make the occasion memorable. This is a good time to read and discuss Ezra Jack Keat's heartwarming book *The Snowy Day,* which is about how a little boy spent all day outside in the snow. Check the Internet for additional ideas on games and activities that will reinforce learning in a fun way.

The next morning, ask your child to participate in home-based physical education by helping mom and dad shovel the snow from the driveway.

# Tell your child your favorite childhood stories

As a storyteller, I have come to understand that children don't like to be preached at. When you try to advise them, they often tune you out. But when you begin to tell them stories, they are more likely to listen to you. They will pay particular attention to stories about your life. Why not tell your child some of the fears you had when you were in second grade? Why not tell him about the day you got a zero on your assignment? Why not tell him the day the bully in your class was giving you a hard time and how you finally put a stop to it in a non-violent way? Tell him how you handled peer pressure in school and in your neighborhood. Your child will be thrilled to hear that, even as adults, you still have to deal with peer pressure, which is commonly called "keeping up with the Joneses."

Through a story, discuss how to avoid being bullied in school or how to avoid getting zeroes on assignments. When you're sharing your experiences this way, you're not preaching. You're discussing the morals of your life story. So, don't be shy. Tell your child about your weaknesses and your strengths when you were a student. Your child will eat it up.

# Use weekends and school holidays for out-of-town trips with your child

Your child cannot afford to miss a whole day of school, never mind a whole week or two of school. Yes, the teachers may give you assignments that classmates may cover, but it's not the same as your child being there as the class learns a new subject or material and then solves problems based on it. It's not easy for a child to do it on his own, so out-of-town trips and long holidays should be planned during the summer or when school is not in session so your child is not harmed academically.

# Verify that your child is actually sleeping when it is bedtime

When my two daughters were growing up, they loved reading, and I would have to check their rooms at night to make sure the lights were not on. You should be aware of all the electronics your child has in his room. You don't want to think that he is sleeping when he is actually watching television, chatting away on the cell phone, or playing on the computer.

A good night's sleep is important to learning. If your child gets a good night's sleep, he will wake up in the morning and be ready to learn when at school. Also, a good night's sleep prevents crankiness, which may get your child into trouble at school.

# Watch the company your child keeps

There's a saying that we become whom we hang out with. You have to know your child's friends, what their goals and priorities are, whether or not they are focused on doing well in school, who their parents are, and their parents' goals and priorities. Don't assume they share your values. People that your child interacts with can influence your child's attitude and beliefs.

# EXtra volunteer time at your child's school helps everyone

When you volunteer at your child's school or in the classroom, you make your presence felt in the school. As your child sees you participating in school activities, he will know that education is very important in your family. It will also send a message to the teachers and the principal that you're serious about the academic success of your child.

If your child gets into trouble, someone will tell you instead of taking him to the principal's office where it would become a bigger issue. You're able to nip any misbehavior in the bud because you're informed. You're told at the beginning, "Johnny did not behave well in school today." You can talk to Johnny, and you can find out whether there's a change in his behavior the following week because you'll probably be at the school.

# You have the most important influence on your child's education

Your child is watching you. For example, you tell your child that reading is important, but has she seen you reading a book? Do you use a library card? It's similar to telling your child not to smoke, but you smoke. She will not believe you. You tell your child that education is important, but are you excited about learning? Are you excited about reading a new book? Your child will pick up this enthusiasm (or lack of it) from you.

# Zero in on the basics of learning: reading, writing, and arithmetic

I've learned over the years that these basics should be emphasized. Make sure that your child loves reading. When your child loves reading, he becomes a good writer. When he uses math in everyday problems, he becomes good at math.

To become highly successful, a person has to be above average in reading, writing, and arithmetic.

Being poor in or doing less in one aspect of the three will make career success more difficult. Many careers require students to be above average in all three disciplines. They're all interrelated. Some children may want to be engineers, but they say, "Uh oh, I'm poor in math." Some may want to be lawyers, but they remember that they're not good in writing. Being above average in all three areas also gives your child a competitive advantage in his chosen field. For example, an engineer who also knows how to write well will go further than one who does not.

Your child should have options. He should be able to choose any profession that he wants to study. Knowing this will empower him.

# About the Author

Dr. Otaigbe's love of learning started at a very young age when he caused a stir in his Nigerian town of Iruekpen on the first day of school in 1960 - he left home to sign up for first grade without his parents' knowledge.

Since he was not quite six years old, his parents had gone to the farm that day, as they usually would. But upon seeing his peers being brought to school, little Otaigbe said to himself, "How about me? I am going to school too." So he got ready, and off he went to school, by himself. After successfully counting to ten and reciting the ABCs, he was admitted to first grade at St. Paul's Primary School. Meanwhile, his mother came back from the farm and no one knew where her son was. Distraught, she searched everywhere until someone suggested she check out the school. That's where she found her son - in the front row of Mr. Imomion's first grade class.

In 1977, almost two decades later, Dr. Otaigbe arrived in the United States and stayed with his former second grade teacher, Dr. Isaac Elimimian. With Dr. Elimimian's encouragement, Dr. Otaigbe graduated valedictorian of his 1979 class at Strayer University. He went on to receive a Master's from Catholic University of America and a Doctorate from American University. He served as Academic Dean of the Woodbridge campus of Strayer University for twenty-four years.

For the past eleven years, Dr. Otaigbe has served on the Prince William County School Board, Virginia. In 2014, he was voted in as Chairman of the Governors' School at Innovation Park, an advanced science and mathematics program which he had proposed be created for high school students.

Dr. Otaigbe and his wife practice what they preach. All their children, Courage, Linda, and Anthony, received their Bachelor's degrees by their eighteenth birthdays. Both Courage and Linda earned their law degrees at age twenty-three from the University of Pennsylvania and University of Virginia, respectively. Anthony earned his Masters in Accounting from George Mason University in December 2014 at age 20.

Dr. Otaigbe credits the guidelines in this book as contributing to the academic success of his children. He adds that these guidelines are not easy to practice, but they work. He believes children are born geniuses, and with dedication and focus, we can nurture the innate, extraordinary abilities of all children.